BORLAND
COUNTRY

Forget that second-ticking clock. Time is the seed
Waiting to fly from the milkweed pod. Time is the speed
Of a dragonfly. Time is the weight of the ripened nut
Eager to fall. Time is the rabbit's desperate scut.
Time's dimensions are hidden in rocks,
In wind and rain, but never in clocks.

BORLAND COUNTRY

by Hal Borland

with photographs by

Walter Chandoha

J. B. LIPPINCOTT COMPANY

Philadelphia and New York

Text copyright © 1947, 1948, 1949, 1950, 1951,
1952, 1953, 1955, 1956, 1971 by Hal Borland
Illustrations copyright © 1971 by Walter Chandoha
All rights reserved
Second Printing
Printed in the United States of America
Library of Congress Catalog Card No.: 72–154846
ISBN–0–397–00738–8

These essays originally appeared on the editorial
page of *The New York Times*. My thanks to the
editor, John B. Oakes, for permission to use
them here.

FOREWORD

This book is about a leisurely year out beyond the centers of urban life, out in what we usually call "the country." Out where there are meadows and pastures and woodlands and fields; and if you look, you will be surprised at how much country there still is in the United States. The last time the figures were tallied up, something like eighty-odd per cent of the people in the U.S. lived on less than two per cent of the total land area. We have become so thoroughly urbanized, even metropolized, that we tend to think there is nothing left but cities and their airports and the throughways that connect them to each other.

But I am not arguing about where people live. All I am trying to say is that there is more unmetropolized countryside than most people think, and that life does go on there. And that is what this book is about. It isn't about any specific year, though. What it has to say is true of every year. Everything that happens in it has happened before and will happen again. There are sunrises and sunsets and full moons and starry nights. Migrant birds come and go. Buds open and flowers bloom and seeds ripen and leaves blaze into autumn color. Trees stand naked to the winter storms. Foxes bark, woodchucks hibernate, whippoorwills call and crows possess the valley in December. Brooks purl, rivers roll, and the silent wedge of ice pries the granite ledges apart. In short, this earth which mothered mankind goes about its business without bothering about minutes or microseconds, or even a calendar.

I am not quite sure what the earth's business is, but I know it is not the nurturing of *Homo sapiens,* or any one species of animal or plant. Certainly the earth, the whole complexity of environmental factors, is not devoted to man's welfare. He is here on sufferance, like any other living thing.

But while we are here, there is a world to know and enjoy as only mankind can enjoy life. That is what this book is about, primarily. The text is about what I have seen and heard and smelled and tasted, and the pictures are of things a photographer has seen and sensed. Perhaps others will see more or differently; but that, too, is the purpose here—to persuade and encourage the reader to look for himself and make his own findings. Too many of us go through life without really looking, blind to the world around us.

The world presented here is not any one place, just as the time is not one particular year. It is here and yonder, and it is over the next hill and just beyond the near horizon. It is not the valley where I live, and yet it is something seen from here simply because there is a common focus for so many of these subjects. Perhaps this is best explained in these words I once wrote about this place:

"The same sun rises here as in Miami or Chicago or Seattle, and the same moon, the same star patterns. My river, like all rivers, flows from an upland to the sea. My valley, like all valleys, has a hill on either side. Mine are global winds, and my rains and snows come from remote sources. My rabbits and squirrels and deer and porcupines are not strange, antipodean creatures; my robins and orioles and wood thrushes and mourning doves are known in the Carolinas and in Ohio and in Arkansas. The equinoxes and solstices are as faithful in coming here as elsewhere."

It is, of course, about the countryside, since it is primarily about enduring matters—enduring, that is, in the sense that you can go back and find them, over and over again. Grass endures, and trees, and a summer sky and winter's snow. Go to the right place at the right time and you will find them in any year.

From time to time when I have written thus about the country someone has said the essays were "nostalgic." Inevitably such a comment has been made by a city person. In the sense that they might provoke a wish to return to a world of apparent simplicities, perhaps there is truth in the nostalgic characterization; but in the sense that they describe a vanished past, it is wholly in error. Such simplicities as I have written about may have been lost and forgotten by the apartment-hermit, but they are fresh and persistent as dawn and daylight out beyond the metropolitan periphery.

Actually, even the most confirmed urbanite cannot completely alienate himself from nature and the outdoors in his artificial environment. All cities have their birds, their insects, their skulking animal life, their insistent weeds and wild plants, all merely waiting for man to turn his back and close his eyes for a season or two. Then they will quietly reclaim the city for their own. All cities have wind and weather, no matter how completely their buildings may be insulated and air-conditioned. And just beyond that urban periphery lies the countryside, even though it may be ignored and even denied. It can be a refuge. More often, and more painfully, it is a reminder that man really is a minority member in the vast community of life on this earth.

Perhaps because these essays were written with these things in mind they are at times uncomfortably nostalgic to those who remember another, somewhat simpler way of life than the urban pressures now impose. But they certainly are not paeans to the past or hymns of homesickness for a lost world. If there is music in them it is the song of the wind in the birches, the pines and the maples and the chorus of orioles and tanagers and robins saluting the summer dawn. It is words and music that persist just over the hill and beyond the throughway. It is the song of time, of the seasons that make up the years of forever, out beyond the fevers and the frenzies of the steel and concrete canyons.

Salisbury, Conn.   H. B.
1971

BORLAND
COUNTRY

A SEED AND AN EQUINOX

No one will deny the wonders and magnificence of astronomy, one of the great sciences which endure as a monument to man's powers of reason and observation. But the annual recurrence of the vernal equinox makes one aware of hidden forces so accurate and so sensitive that the observer can scarcely escape a feeling of awe and wonder. All around one are the evidences of sensitivity to time and the stars that make any human science pall a little by contrast.

Man has known for a long time the fixed sequence of star and planet, earth, sun, moon and tides. But how can a seed "know" when to begin to sprout? How can sap at the roots of a tree "know" when comes the proper time to start that mysterious movement upward toward twig and waiting leaf-bud? What moves a bulb to muster forces and send up shoots to catch the sunlight and begin to manufacture food for the plant? What mysterious force prompts one seed to wait in its sprouting till all danger of frost is past, while another sprouts at that precise moment when its stem and leaf can survive ten degrees of frost but not twelve or fifteen?

We have answers, of a sort, in terms of warmth and length of daylight; but those are, in final examination, observations of response, not of ultimate cause. We have elaborate apparatus to measure sun's warmth and soil's moisture and even sap pressure. But how does a grass seed measure such critical conditions? Somehow they are measured by all living things which spread leaves and manufacture chlorophyll. They "know" when the equinox comes, when spring arrives, when they should respond. Man studies a clock and a star to learn such basic simplicities.

MARCH VISITORS

Youngsters may believe it when they are told that pussy willows appear in earliest spring simply to show off their warm fur coats. But the real reason is that *Salix discolor*, as the botanists call it, is a hardy shrub with early habits. It isn't so forward as the witch hazel, which blooms in the fall; but it pretty well sets the pace for all the spring shrubs.

The "pussy," of course, is not the blossom. It is the bud, from which the outer scales have fallen. The true blossoms come a few weeks later, changing the silvery catkin to a more ragged tuft of yellowish miniature flowers. Staminate and pistillate flowers are borne on different trees, as with all the willows. And when the flowers have done their duty, with the help of the early bees, then the leaves appear.

All willows have catkins, of one form or another, and many of the lesser willow trees, particularly the shrubs that fringe the streams and swamps, can compete in a lesser way with the pussy willows. Even the bearberry willow, which creeps on the windy slopes of the eastern mountains and seldom lifts its branches more than a foot off the ground, has furry little catkins. So does the even smaller dwarf willow, *Salix herbacea*, which lives on the mountain summits. The really big willows, white, black, crack, and weeping, have catkins that vary from furry little tufts to long, slender plumes. And they all bloom early.

If pussy willows didn't appear until May they would hardly get a second glance. In March they get praise and a hearty welcome.

APPRAISAL

April, when spring is just beginning, is a good time to appraise it as a season. And without either sentiment or sentimentality, which inevitably creep in about the time that violets bloom and apple blossoms scent the air. It's a good time to be matter of fact about spring, because we are not yet engulfed in it.

Spring is one of those things that man has no hand in, any more than he has a part in sunrise or the phases of the moon. It is more difficult to believe this when the yard is full of daffodils that you planted last summer; but it's true, nevertheless. You can't fend off an April frost, and you can't make a daffodil bulb grow by holding it in your hand or carrying it around in your pocket. You have to put it in the ground, and trust to forces beyond human power or control.

Spring came before man was here to enjoy it, and it will go right on coming even if man isn't here some time in the future. It is a matter of solar mechanics and celestial order. And for all our knowledge of astronomy and terrestrial mechanics, we can't alter the arrival of the spring equinox by as much as one second.

Spring is a matter of growth, of chlorophyll, of bud and blossom. We can alter growth and change the time of blossoming, in individual plants; but the forests still grow in nature's way, and the grass of the plains hasn't altered its nature in a thousand years.

Spring is a magnificent phase of the cycle of nature; but man really hasn't any guiding or controlling hand in it. He just happens to be here, to enjoy it and benefit by it. And this is a good time to realize it. By May, we will want to take full credit.

THE ROOT OF THE MATTER

This is the season when one can listen only so long to any recital of the world's shortcomings. Then we have to get outdoors and see the world itself. There we know that though a thousand things may be wrong, a million things are right.

What are some of them? They are so obvious it seems foolish to list them. Water still runs downhill, making brooks that sing. Grass sends up new shoots, greening hillside and meadow. Robins migrate and strut about the lawn and sing their mating call. Daffodils swell in bud and open petals that are more yellow than gold. Weeping willows turn green and graceful while maples put forth their wine-red blossoms. The new-turned earth of field or garden is still full of fertility. Ferns send up pale green fiddleheads. Bees begin their summer's search. The man of the soil prepares his fields and sorts his seeds, knowing that the earth is eager to nourish another crop.

These are simple, obvious things. They may be seen any April, along with the swelling of apple buds and the opening of tulips. If they happened but once in ten years we would wait breathless for their coming, and put aside all other worries for their arrival. Instead, they are commonplace and taken for granted while we bandy words and dispute ideas. The trouble is that the words are too often rootless and the ideas are sterile. Who can command a man to plant hemp and harvest wheat—or to plant hate and harvest peace? Who can command a lark to sing the oriole's song?

The world is in order, out where ideas have roots. April invites a conference on an open hillside to investigate the state of things at their common source.

14

THE MOMENT

The year holds one moment, which may last for a week, when tree and bush and vine are on the breathless verge of leafing out. It is then that you stand on a hillside and look across the wooded valley and see the scarlet and orange of maple blossoms like a touch of pastel crayon across the treetops. You see the greenish yellow in the tops of the wineglass elms, and the amber green fountain that is the big weeping willow beside the brook.

These generalities, so to speak, you see at a glance; and you know the breathless moment is here. Then you look at particulars. The crab apple trees in the orchard are dressed in green lace, their leaves no larger than your little fingernail. The lilacs are all tufted at their stem ends, each leaf cluster tipped with faint brownish purple and not a leaf among them as big as a squirrel's ear. The wild blackberries have scarlet tassels not half an inch long, each tassel an unfolding group of leaves whose form can already be faintly seen. The late apple trees have gray silver nubs at their twig tips; draw down a branch and look closely and you see each nub as a young leaf cluster emerging from its bud, each leaf the size of a ladybug's wing and each red-tipped as though blushing. The privet has a leaf tuft like a miniature green magnolia, and the bridal wreath bush is green at every joint with little green rosebud leaves.

These things you see now, this instant. An hour from now all will be changed; tomorrow it will be still different. For this is the trembling moment when life stands between bud and leaf, between promise and achievement. A new world is in the making on these old, old hills, even as we watch.

BEYOND

*E*ver since the first spring that ever was, man stood at this season with awe in his eyes and wonder in his heart, seeing the magnificence of life returning and life renewed. And something deep responded, whatever his religion or spiritual belief. It is as inevitable as sunrise that man should see the substance of faith and hope in the tangible world so obviously responding to forces beyond himself or his accumulated knowledge.

For all his learning and sophistication, man still instinctively reaches toward that force beyond, and thus approaches humility. Only arrogance can deny its existence, and the denial falters in the face of evidence on every hand. In every tuft of grass, in every bird, in every opening bud, there it is. We can reach so far with our explanations, and there still remains a force beyond which touches not only the leaf, the seed, the opening petal, but man himself.

Spring is a result, not a cause. The cause lies beyond, still beyond. And it is the instinctive knowledge of this which inspires our festivals of faith and life and belief renewed. Resurrection is there for us to witness and participate in; but the resurrection around us still remains the symbol, not the ultimate truth. And men of good will instinctively reach for truth—beyond the substance of spring, of a greening and revivifying earth, of nesting and mating and birth, of life renewed. Thus we come to Easter, and all the other festivals of faith, celebrating life and hope and the ultimate substance of belief—reaching, like the leaf itself, for something beyond, ever beyond.

A BOY AND A BROOK

Travel the country roads on a weekend, when school is not in session, particularly the hill roads beside the brooks, and you will see him. The boy beside the brook, the boy with a bait rod or a fly rod and a special light in his eye. Note that it isn't a willow pole he has, nor a twine string with a bent pin. Chances are you can look all season long and never see that fictional young fisherman. If he ever did exist, which is doubtful, he is gone now. This boy beside the brook isn't being picturesque; he's fishing. He probably has a nylon line, and he knows his leaders, his wet flies and dry ones, and the way to use a worm. He also knows the water, the coves, the eddies, the ripples, and he knows fish.

Country boys have been fishing for a long, long time. It's a part of their growing up. Listen to a middle-aged man in waders and within five minutes he will say, "When I was a boy" or "Thirty years ago," and tell you the exciting things that happened right over at that bend or at the mouth of that brook. He has special memories, and now and then he will even share them. Not only of fish and fishing, but of sunlight on water, and shad-blow in bloom, and misty dawns, and days that were full of April, or May, or June.

If you ever wondered why fishing is probably the most popular sport in this country, watch that boy beside the brook and you will learn. If you are really perceptive you will. For he already knows that fishing is only one part fish. Unless you too were a fisherman when you were young you may never know the other components, but you can sense them a little, just watching. That boy probably won't tell you. He's a little bashful about such things. But he will remember, all his years. And so will you, just seeing him, seeing that look in his eyes.

THE LITTLE ROSES

If an appleblossom is like a wild rose in miniature, it is no accident, but rather a kinship of the kind which links many strange cousins. The rose, the apple, the pear, the chokecherry, even the shadbush, all belong to the same botanical family. And if one wishes for more thorny kin, add the hawthorns in all their variations. They are all roses, of one kind or another.

The apple is old in its own right. Prehistoric man ate apples, on scientific evidence, and even cultivated apple trees. And, being man, he no doubt enjoyed the beauty of their blossoms. Quite probably, prehistoric woman wore appleblossoms in her hair. On Biblical evidence, we know that woman early knew the taste of the fruit, and chose to share it.

Examine an appleblossom. It is, indeed, a small rose, five-petaled and full of fragrance. Its bud was the same as that of a wild rose, and as the sepals opened it had the lovely color on the furled petals that marks the rose slowly opening in the brambly corner of the pasture fence. It, too, has the many stamens of the rose, which are cinnamon-tipped. And it has a fragrance like that of a wild rose slightly spiced and touched with cider. Watch it through the season, and the appleblossom becomes a hip, like that of the rose but bigger, meatier, more sweet to the taste.

There they stand now, the little roses on the apple trees, great bouquets of small petals, buzzing with bees on a sunny afternoon, sweetening every breeze, flushed with their own simple beauty.

THE FERNS

Fiddleheads uncurl and the bright new fronds of the ferns begin to spread themselves at the foot of the banks where violets and Dutchman's-breeches are full of bloom. If there is something venerable and touched with mystery in the uncurling of a fern, there is reason, for the ferns are literally as old as most of the hills. Their beginnings go back millions of years, and fern fossils found in the ancient rocks show little difference from those now opening in the warm May sun. Counterparts of lady ferns and maidenhair, wood ferns and cinnamon ferns grew here in the days when our mountains were still mud flats washed by the young, restless oceans.

For generations men were baffled by the ferns, which bore no flowers and had no seeds, yet throve and multiplied. Ferns were magic plants, and those who dealt in magic believed that if they could only find the seed of a fern they would have the ultimate in mysterious power. They never found a fern "seed," of course, for ferns multiply by a complex of spores and intermediate growth in the form of prothallium. It is a process that requires seven years from spore to mature fern, and it goes on so secretly that few are aware of it.

Yet ferns are everywhere. In some size or form they grow in almost every region of the world. And every spring they come nosing from the leaf mold along our roadsides and in our woodlands, common as violets, yet still overlaid with their ancient air of mystery. Like the very old and very wise of our own race, they seem to have outgrown haste and impatience and the need for sharing secrets.

SENSORY SEASON

There is a sweetness of May verging on June that no other time in the whole year can equal. And by sweetness is meant more than flower fragrance or honey taste; this is the greater sweetness of understanding and emotion, the glow of pleasure in being.

This is the sensory season. Trees are in leaf, even the cautious oaks and the casual hickories. It is a green world, full of elusive fragrances. Walk through an orchard and you can smell as well as feel the strength of grass underfoot, new grass reaching tall toward the sun. Boughs naked only a little while ago, then bright and heady with bloom, now rustle with leaf and tingle with the strength of fruition. Listen, and you can almost hear the pulse of sap and the mysterious workings of chlorophyll.

The hills are rounded with their own green growth, the soft hills of a lush and friendly land. The valleys sing with brooks, laughing waters of spring and seep that have not yet felt the thirst of summer. Even the stone walls are alive with vine, the creeping tendrils of life that would root in granite and suck faint sustenance from sandstone.

The air vibrates with bird song, which is the great rhythm made palpable to the human ear. The oriole's rounded notes are as delightful to the ear as the tanager's bright scarlet is delightful to the eager eye. All the senses tingle, alive with the season as the world itself is alive. Nothing is impossible at such a time. High achievement is all around us, beating on every sense for recognition.

REDISCOVERY

We seldom remember in April how tall the grass at the roadside and in the meadows will be by June. Or that daisies will frost the fence row and buttercups gild the meadow. We forget, most of us, that choke-cherries are now in bloom with their sharp-tanged flowers, and that June is other things than roses.

June is really a time of relative quiet, serenity after the rush of sprouting and leafing and flowering and before the fierce heat that drives toward maturity and seed. June's very air can be as sweet as the wild strawberries that grace its middle weeks, sweet as clover, sweet as honeysuckle. A sweetness that could be cloying, but somehow isn't, perhaps because it is still a new sweetness.

Birds still sing at their best, and not only at morn and at evening but most of the day. The oriole, the robin and the tanager can make a June day fairly vibrate with song, and a part of the song is there in the air before the birds utter a single note. June is that way. The rasping that is July and August, the scraping of cicadas and all their kin, is yet in abeyance. June doesn't assault your ears. It flatters them, then softens the sound of frog and whippoorwill, and is a joy.

These things we know each June. We learn them all over again in the first week, and we wonder how we could ever have forgotten them. For June is peonies as well as roses, June is the first early kitchen-garden produce as well as flower beds, June is a happy memory rediscovered and lived again.

ESSENCE OF JUNE

*T*he man who mows the lawn gave us the season's first whiff of that sweet, green fragrance of fresh-cut grass; but now come the haymakers, and the whole countryside takes on a fragrance as characteristic of June as the fragrance of lilacs is of May. The mowers clatter, the tall grass falls in windrows, and the haymaking is on.

June haymaking used to be a hazardous necessity because of June rain. But not any more. Ingenious technologists got to work and turned out hay choppers and hay driers and a lot of other equipment. Nowadays the farmers stow their early hay green, chopped and fresh, in silos. There it undergoes a process known as ensilage, a fermentation which preserves and even enhances the nourishment and flavor of growing things—to a cow, at least. The mowers start in the hay fields right after breakfast, the rakes soon follow, the chopper follows the rakes, the trucks follow the chopper, and before dusk the hay is in the silo.

Or, if the farmer insists on dry hay from his first crop, he can dry it a bit on the ground, bale it and stow it in a loft equipped with a drier which will cure it safely even in the midst of a wet spell. Dry hay, however, usually comes from a later cutting.

Whatever the ultimate purpose, now the mowers go to work in the hay fields. The brome, the timothy, the clover, the alfalfa are cut, and the sweetness pervades the valleys. Not a hay smell; just the fresh-cut green smell. The hay smell is a further distillation, with sunshine in it, and dew, and a touch of wild mint, and just a trace of buttercup. The essence not only of hay, but of June. A summer smell if there ever was one!

THE QUIET FISHERMAN

There are all kinds of fishermen, as well as persons who do not fish at all. Probably the most baffling of the cult are the still-fishermen, those who spend hours in a small boat or on the bank with a bamboo pole or a bait rod, apparently sitting in the sun with no pressing purpose, no worries, no energy. Nonfishermen shake their heads in bafflement. Fly-fishermen smile and shake their heads. But the still-fishermen go right on fishing, for perch and big sunfish, and bullheads, and even the lowly rock bass. Pan fishing, some call it; they fish not only to catch fish, but to eat them. And they usually fish with worms for bait.

Still-fishermen are generally quiet, patient folk with a touch of poetry in their souls. They seldom talk about it, but there is something soothing and reassuring in a riverbank or a pond, at dawn, at dusk, or even at midday when the fish seldom bite. They know the quiet waters, those still-fishermen, and the look of a mud turtle on a log, the quick beat of a kingfisher's wings, the flash of a dragonfly. They know sunrise and sunset. They know the hidden coves, the peaceful places. They know where a man can have an hour's meditation between bites as well as where he can be kept so busy he has no time for thought or worry.

Fishing is not all catching fish, by any means; but it is well to come home with your supper. And what better supper for any fisherman than a couple of yellow perch? Some may argue the point, but few of the dissenters will be still-fishermen; for most of them agree that any man's choice is his own catch. Worm-fishing breeds individualism and tolerance in about equal proportions. No bait rod was ever used to pound an opinion into a dissenter's head.

THE FLOW OF TIME

You can sit on a lawn or under a tree now and almost see the way time flows past. It doesn't hurry or dawdle; it simply flows, much as a great cumulus cloud moves across the summer sky. You can feel it, somehow, too, if you don't try too hard. In growing things, mostly. In the way a leaf turns to catch the sun, the way a bud opens and the petals uncurl into a rose, the way a bean flower fades and the green pod forms.

Time isn't a tangible. And yet you can touch so many things that mean time and continuity. There is a kind of time in a seed, for instance. Plant a radish seed, and in a few weeks you can eat a radish. Plant an acorn, and an oak, for the centuries, may grow. There is another kind of time in a brook, which carves its channel and yet is shaped by stones; and, in due time, it wears away the stones. It floods and it ebbs, but so long as there are rains and the hills slope downward the brook will continue to flow.

And there are times when time is like the wind, seeming to howl at the corners and lash at human habitations. Troubled times, mostly; times of personal crises. But crises pass, and time, like the wind, comes back to normal. And one can sit on the lawn at evening and watch the infinite grace of the swallows in the air and smell the fragrance of the roses and the honeysuckle, and hear the soft whisper of approaching night in the big elms. Time flows then, as it should, not hour by hour but season by season and year by year. The long flow is there, and if one does not watch too closely or listen too intently, one will see and hear.

MEADOW FROST

Daisies gleam along the untrimmed roadsides and stand in drifts of white at the fence corners. Some call them Farmer's Curse, but they are flowers of the chrysanthemum family. The common field daisy, often called oxeye daisy, is botanically *Chrysanthemum leucanthemum*, and it is cousin of the herb feverfew, which was brought from Europe long ago and naturalized into our gardens.

The name "daisy" reaches far back into history. It comes from the Old English, directly from the term "day's eye." But the flower known as a daisy in England is not our oxeye daisy at all. It has fleshy stem and leaves and flowers with colored petals. We sometimes grow it in our gardens under the name "English daisy."

Our field daisy is a composite, of the same big family as the sunflowers, and the yellow disk at its center is, as in all such Compositae, made up of a mass of tiny individual flowers. One needs a magnifying glass to see these florets in their miniature beauty, but there they are, each a complete flower and all of them packed together into a golden disk. Each of them, when the flower matures, produces its seed. Pull off the white rays, or petals, from a daisy and the disk you have left is a good deal like the flower head of the common tansy, which has no rays at all.

Like so many of the wildlings, daisies are too common for their own good. If they were as rare as arbutus, they would be treasured and exclaimed over and even glorified. Even their foliage would be properly appreciated, for it is both beautiful and graceful. But few give it a second glance.

MILKWEED

The botanical name is Asclepias, honoring Aesculapius, the Greek god of healing. The everyday name is milkweed, and the two best-known members of the family, butterfly weed and common milkweed, are now in bloom. Butterfly weed lifts its showy orange flower head in favored places. The common milkweed is everywhere, less spectacular with its tassely tufts of lavender and white florets, but full of sweetness, a subtle mixture of tuberose and honeysuckle fragrance.

Roadside weed though it is, the milkweed has virtues beyond a pretty flower and a sweet scent. Its milky sap contains caoutchouc, the raw material of rubber, which periodically attracts scientific searchers for source materials. Fibers of the stem have been used for cordage. Fluff from the seed pod has been used to stuff pillows; the silky fibers lack the natural twist, however, that would make them valuable for thread or yarn. Both roots and juice have been in the herbalist's stock for generations, particularly for respiratory ills. And the fresh shoots in early May make palatable cooked greens.

The common milkweed's florets are fertilized chiefly by the bees. Those florets occur in tufts of seventy or more, each less than a quarter of an inch in diameter; and each, by one of those quirks of nature, is a trap for the kind of insect which fertilizes it and thus insures the perpetuation of the species. One misstep, and the bee or ant is caught by a leg and doomed to a starving death. Yet for untold centuries bees have fertilized milkweed and ants have done their part, never learning. For insects never learn, it seems, perhaps because their lives are too short to do more than obey simple compulsion and instinct. And so the milkweed survives and thrives and multiplies, and the world is a somewhat sweeter place.

THUNDERSTORM

There is an awesome majesty about a July thunderstorm, particularly if one is safe under shelter; and an ideal shelter is a house on a hillside, facing a span of hills and valleys, for the drama of such a storm lies in its approach.

The day has been hot, humid. Toward evening the sky darkens. Clouds mass on the farther hills. They approach, full of turbulent motion. There is a hush, in which even a bird cry seems much too loud. Trees wait in the breathless air. Then there is a stir across the valley. You can see the riffling in the treetops long before you can hear the swish of the wind. The clouds come closer.

Lightning flashes, back in the hills. You count the seconds before the thunder rolls over you. Another flash, closer this time. The second ridge is blotted out. In the pause, the wind sweeps into the valley. The birds are quiet now, but the valley trees bow and their swish becomes a roar. You wince at the lightning.

The darkness has turned to gray on the second ridge. The gray marches toward you, creeps down the first ridge; and you hear the rush of rain, the pelt and swish and lesser roar. Trees sway under it. Thunder booms, drowning the roar of the rain.

The first ridge is veiled in rain, gray, streaming. The valley quivers under the rain, the trees trembling. Rain creeps up the hillside. Then here it is, upon you, just outside the window; and the sky loses its darkness. It is almost silvery with rain-gleam.

Rain sheets down, begins to thin away. The long light of late sun touches the second ridge. The air is cooled. The storm passes. The thunder rumbles in the distance, retreating, dying away.

THE INDIVIDUALISTS

Sometimes they are called "escapes," sometimes "volunteers." The name doesn't matter. They are tough, hardy independents which have adapted themselves to a hard way of life and which thrive and reproduce not only without the help of gardener or farmer but often in the face of his opposition. Most of them are flowers—petunias, phlox, balsam, flowering tobacco, day lilies, an occasional hollyhock; but some are vegetables and shrubs—the stray lilacs, the barberry that grows in old pastures, even the asparagus that lifts its ferny plume beside the country road. There are many, and they are persisent, and the broadminded gardener has to admire them for their vigor and independence.

To the neat gardener and the methodical farmer they are weeds. They don't belong where they are, and they don't reproduce true to pattern, the pattern imposed upon them by the hybridists. They revert, phlox to the distasteful magenta, for instance. But they do develop a hardiness, to drought and heat and insect pests, that the plant breeder sometimes finds useful; and on occasion they produce sports, new variants, and back to the gardens they come. Thus they do have their occasional value even to those who disdain them.

But their chief virtue is perhaps symbolic in a world of persistent conformity. They go their own way, meet conditions as they are and survive by sheer persistence and root-strength. They need no coddling. They choose their own soil and climate. They fight their own battle of survival. There are times when it does a man's heart good to see a rejected phlox or hollyhock or even a petunia blooming in a waste place where all the odds are against success.

CORN

The smell of corn pollen is like no other fragrance in the world, and here in America it is as typical of August as the crunch of tooth on roasting ear. It is a fragrance, moreover, that predates European settlement here by untold centuries. It hangs heavy now over the land, but it was here when Rome was young.

Despite research and exploration, the origins of our corn are still misted in the remote past. All we know with certainty is that the Indians must have developed it in one of the greatest botanical achievements of all time. It undoubtedly stems from a wild grass, but that grass has been only tentatively identified. Indians of both Americas were growing sweet corn, popcorn and meal corn of various strains when the first Europeans arrived. Long before that it had passed that stage where it would revert to the wild type if left untended. Botanists can make only rough estimates of its age.

The developments of corn since then have been notable, but in comparison with the original development they remain minor. We have altered its appearance slightly, greatly increased its yield, changed its milling qualities. But nubbins found in ancient cliff dwellings of the Southwest can match, feature by feature, nubbins from almost any backyard corn patch of today.

The pollen smell which hangs heavy over much of America now is an old, old fragrance. Go to Australia, or the Argentine, or to Asiatic Russia, or to many flatland fields of Europe, and you will find the same fragrance, in its season. Corn, Indian maize, has become a staple foodstuff of the whole world. Yet its history is as elusive as the pollen smell itself, for it is a history written only in flaked stone implements and botanical speculation.

THE POND

The quiet ponds are scummed over, now, and full of algae; and one gets the feeling that anything could happen in such waters, any kind of life arise from them. Here, in the dead heat of late summer, is the marshy margin and the primordial ooze with cattails growing in it, and he who approaches it might be walking backward in time toward remote beginnings.

Even the pond creatures and those along its margins belong to another time than the present. Of the reptiles, the snapping turtle is one of the ancients, armored like a creature of the Silurian Age and eyeing the world as from the midst of a tree-fern jungle. The frogs are primitives, tadpoles which have shed gills and tails and crept up on land in the venerable cycle of living things from the ooze to the rocks. The water snakes are still slithering through the vanished age when pterodactyls had not yet grown wings. And in the air drift and dart such dragonflies as can be found as fossils in rocks older than coal.

Even the birds that haunt the pond have an otherworldly air, the gaunt herons with their beady eyes and darting beaks, and the bobtailed kingfishers which have neither grace nor particular beauty, for all their quick, spectacular efficiency. They, too, might be creatures of the in-between time, when the land was still rising from the swamps.

The water is green with algae, tepid with mud warmth, a kind of protoplasmic soup full of strange and struggling uncertainties. But the hills look down and the hills are certainty itself, for they are the land risen from the muck, the rock, the soil, the maturity of an age reflected briefly in the stagnant pond.

TOWARD MATURITY

The urgency that was midsummer now begins to relax, and September comes in sight over the land. You see it in the trees, you see it at the roadsides where the uncut weeds begin to reach maturity, and you see it in the fields and pastures. Oat fields are stubble now, the golden grain harvested. Corn stands tall, the ears in silk and filling day by day. The first goldenrod begins to gleam in fence rows where wild asters will soon be taking the place of daisy and black-eyed Susan.

Spring is sprouting, and early summer is the rush of growth and the competition of blooming. But late summer is more sedate; it is fulfillment of time and purpose, the seed, the fruit, for which growth itself was destined. The time of haste is past, the pod, the capsule, the nut, the seed-head already formed and coming to completion. The egg is hatched, the fledgling now on the wing. Even the bees are less urgent in their rounds. Small rabbits scurry at the roadside, well past the nursling stage; and woodchucks, full of sun and succulence, begin to lay on the fat for hibernation.

Hot days are still upon us, but the sun's nooning is from a different angle; and nights lengthen, dusk to dawn. The owl has already spoken in the woodland, and the crows are restless and full of noise. All a part of the pattern, the maturing change that has its own calendar. For who can stay the wind or hasten the apple? Time flows with the season, not the other way round, and the season flows like a river, from its own springs. Summer ripens and matures, even as the fox grape on the riverbank, and August leans toward September and the equinox and autumn.

THE PURPLE TIME

Now come the rich purples in the fields and meadows, denoting not only a time but a maturity. It is as though the whole summer had been building toward this deep, strong color of royalty, to match the gold of late sunlight and early goldenrod.

And that is, in a sense, what has been happening. Flower colors are mysterious, as to cause. It is generally accepted that the full, hot sun of the tropics produces stronger colors, the brilliant golden yellows, the deep oranges, the full-bodied scarlets. It is also understood that the lesser sun of the temperate zone produces lesser colors, for the most part.

Our early spring brings us, except in the violets, the weaker shades, the whites, the pinks, the thin yellows and the light blues. Early summer warms the landscape with yellows and deeper blues, some orange and a variety of reds. But it takes late August and the accumulation of sun and warmth to give us the strength of purple in showy mass.

Here is that purple. The thistles flaunt it, prickly, forbidding, but stout of stem and even more stout of color. The burdock, troublesome weed that it is, reveals its purple tufts which will ripen into hook-spined burrs eager to hitch a ride to new fields. Ironweed stands tall in the lowlands and lifts its massed heads of the warmest purple to the sun. There is a purple to catch any eye, and hold it, a magnificent purple. And the asters now approach their season; the small white ones will frost the countryside, but among them will stand the purple of their own royalty, to be sought out and remembered.

The summer frays away toward September, but it does so in purple majesty, strong, full-bodied, full of summer sun.

MORNING MIST

As August slowly cools away toward autumn, dawns become misty as with a foretaste of the chill ahead. Over the ponds and streams the mist is like smoke, curling and wreathing in the sunrise air as the mysterious little currents of breeze play tag; white smoke, the incense of fading summer, which vanishes as the sun reaches higher above the horizon.

This is not the haze of high humidity which clouds the hills on a sultry midsummer morning. This is the shimmery gauze of the changing season, the dew which washes the dust from the summer-weary leaves along the streams and keeps green the valleys beyond the season's prime. This is the blown breath of autumn long before there is even a hint of frost in the air.

It comes on a morning with a clear sky and a clean horizon, a brilliant morning full of blue and green and the long shadows of sunrise. It is not a gray mist; it is white, white as daisy petals, whiter than cumulus clouds, luminous white and so thin it glistens as the sun strikes through it. It is like spider web jeweled with dew, and even less tangible. Wave a hand and there is a swirl and a quick gleam of sun in mistless air.

Indian summer will come, and the thin, far haze on the hilltops; but this is even less substantial. The haze of Indian summer will be day-long; this is morning mist, sunrise magic which vanishes even while you watch. It is a curl of shimmer, the very essence of impermanence, a swift glimpse of autumn already round the bend of the river and waiting there beyond the hills.

EAT UP!

One who has lived with a garden all summer comes now to the time when a sense of immediacy begins to close in. Days shorten. Growth slackens. The garden is still full and overflowing with plenty, but one knows that it may be the last full crop. The season grows late.

At planting time the season stretched ahead almost without limit. The first fruits were precious, garner from the fertile soil. Midsummer brought bounty. Then so much came at once that there was a surfeit. But now, with an end in sight when the frost will come creeping up the valleys, the garden is precious again.

Corn is at its peak, but will the late corn have time to mature its ears? Early lettuce bolted in the heat; will the late lettuce, now beginning to head, make its way to the salad bowl? Will the scattered blossoms on the limas make pods, or is this present crop to be the last? And what of the string beans and the summer squash? What of the cauliflower—will it, or the frost, win out?

One picks the pods and the ears, pulls the carrots and appraises the beets. One watches the winter squash, and looks for signs of blight on the tomato plants, wondering which of the green tomatoes will ripen. And the flavor, once the garden comes to the table, is almost as good as it was when the first small peas were eaten. The season that was going to last forever begins to fade; days lie ahead when there will be neither pod nor pome in the garden but only dry stalks and frosty ground. Eat up! The end is in sight with September already upon us.

HARVEST MOON

This is the weekend of the harvest moon, which, regardless of calendar or equinox, is autumnal as a corn shock. The full moon doesn't come till tomorrow, but, as reasonably clear skies return, it will be a moonlit weekend. The harvest moon is not a hasty moon; it comes early and stays late.

There was a time when the harvest moon gave the busy farmer the equivalent of an extra day or two. He could return to the fields after supper and evening milking and continue his harvest by moonlight. That was when corn was cut by hand and husked by hand, when shocks teepeed the fields and fodder was stacked in the barnyard, when the song of the bangboard echoed and the huskin' peg was familiar to the hand.

But times change, and schedules. Now most of the farmer's long days come at plowing time, or planting, or hay time. Corn is cut by machine and chopped by machine and stowed in the silo; or it is left standing in the field till a few fine late fall days, then picked by the mechanical picker, which can outstrip a dozen men.

There's harvesting to be done, of course, but much of it now centers on the kitchen rather than the barns. The last bountiful yield comes from the garden—the late sweet corn, the tomatoes, the root vegetables, the dozen-and-one kinds of pickles and relishes. The canning, the freezing, the preserving, the kitchen harvest in all its variety, reaches its busy peak, the last rush of the season.

It's still the harvest moon, but the farmer with his field harvest well in hand is looking forward to the next full moon, the one in October. So is his dog. That will be the hunter's moon, and the coons should still be busy in the cornfields then.

CLIMBING COLOR

The brightest color in the woods these next few weeks will not be on the leaf of a tree or a shrub, but on a vine. On that cousin of the fox grape which the botanists know as *Psedera qinquefolia* and which is sometimes known as woodbine and sometimes as Virginia creeper. Virginia creeper is the better name, though Virginia is only one of thirty or more states where it grows wild and in profusion; woodbine is an English term applied, even in this country, also to various of the honeysuckles.

Any day now the Virginia creeper will begin to flame in the woods. Its leaves turn one of the finest scarlets in nature, and the vine's habit of climbing to the very top of any tree, particularly tall dead ones, makes it a veritable pillar of fire in autumn. You can see a creeper-festooned tree a quarter of a mile away in late September, and no matter how many times you see it you want to stop and admire its amazing beauty.

By some it is mistaken for poison ivy, though identification is easy. As its Latin name indicates, its leaves generally occur in groups of five on a stem; the poison ivy leaves occur in threes and are of a different shape. And the ivy leaves more often turn orange and yellow rather than scarlet. The inconspicuous berries on the ivy, furthermore, are a dull gray; the berries on the Virginia creeper are miniatures of the wild grape and a lively blue.

So there it climbs, generous in leaf and profligate in color, one of the finest of our woods climbers. Only the maple leaf can begin to rival its color, and the maples color a bit later. The creeper doesn't wait. It is beginning to celebrate right now.

THE RIVER

A river in the hill-lands is a beautiful thing at any time of year, but in late September it is a stream of wonder, changing day by day and even hour by hour. That is the wonder of it, the change, the moods reflected and even magnified; and beyond that is the freight, large and small, that it brings from the distant hills and carries silently past to deposit in the lower valleys. The little freight is moving now, the falling leaves and the berries and the myriad winged seeds.

Watch an upland river for an hour and you see autumn flowing past, even before it has a firm hold on the hills. The first red maple leaves are there, and the poplar leaves like golden galleons, prows high, and the broad, papery leaves of fox grape and sycamore. Milkweed floss dances over the slow current, so light it fairly bounces over the water, fluff that will lose its buoyancy in time and float to some shallow to root and make more floss for another autumn. Even thistledown, set free by the energetic feeding of a late goldfinch, floats here in the light drift of air above the water, shimmery gauze that too will be borne to some new rootground. Pokeberries, ink-black, and purple viburnums and the gray berries of red-osier dogwood drift past on broken stems, freed by a gusty wind or a browsing cow or a deer upstream.

The willows nod gently at their soft reflections and loose a few yellowed leaves, as in tribute. A late flight of infinitely small white moths skims the water, skipping like the thistledown. A terrapin slides from an old log with a soft splash. Autumn, slowly staining the woodland, is there on the river, its colors flowing down from the hills where it gathers strength to take over the valleys.

PUT AWAY THAT HOE

This is the time of year when a vegetable garden needs a frost. The gardener himself secretly wishes for a frost, though it isn't quite cricket to come right out and say so. Openly he is expected to brag about the tomatoes he still has ripening. Actually, he has ripened just about enough tomatoes for this year. He is willing to call it quits and wait for May and radishes and tomato plants. By then he will be fed up with canned tomatoes, and he knows it; by then he would pay a dollar apiece for those greenish-orange tomatoes now on his vines. But right now he'll settle for a clean-up job in the garden and a weekend without a hoe, a spray gun or a duster in his hands.

That's one of the best things about nature in a land of four seasons—frost comes and puts an end to the succulent growing things. No garden should endure, with all its dividends and demands, more than about six months a year. The other six months one should be allowed to rest and dream and yearn and get rid of the calluses. And think how wonderful is modern transportation, which brings fresh garden produce from California and Texas and Florida. And think loftily how much better home-grown lettuce and beans and corn and tomatoes are than those thus miraculously transported. Six months, as it were, to appreciate.

Hail the frost! Hail the blackened vine! Let those who make green-tomato pickles have those green tomatoes! The corn stands sere and stripped, the beans are rustling in the wind, the death rattle in their dried pods. The squash have given up. The lettuce has all bolted. Put away the hoe, close the garden gate, and let it frost.

TANG AND TINT

When the leaves begin to take on color in the mass, there's a scientific explanation for the change which has to do with the chemistry of plant life as well as the facts of botany. Frost has nothing to do with it, of course; it's a matter of oxidation, of pigmentation, of chemical change. And that's all very well to know. But there's a rule of tongue, as one might say, which is also worth knowing, and that is that the really colorful leaves of autumn are those of shrubs and trees which have sugar in their sap or tannin in their make-up.

The maples, most vivid of all the woodland's trees, are the sweetest of all when the sap is running. Sweet gum, which has a warm, sweet juice in midsummer, runs the maples a close second. Sour gum, which some call tupelo, has a sweet tang to its sap and a rainbow of color to its leaves. Sassafras, which has sweetness as well as an old familiar flavor, splashes the woods with its variegated autumn finery. The oaks, traditional source of tannin, are the bearers of the strongest reds and the deepest purples in the autumn hills. Fruit trees, too, which have a special sweetness of sap, run to colorful leaves, though they are less reluctant to let them fall.

Go down the list and test them with the tongue and the eye, season by season. If the sap is sweet the autumn leaves will tend to gold and crimson, and if the sap is pungent and full of the taste of tannin the leaves will show deep red and even purple. Perhaps it's only another way of getting at the facts of science without actually stating them, but the tang and the tint have their relationship for the tongue to taste and the eye to see.

OCTOBER

 *B*lond October comes striding over the hills wearing a crimson shirt and faded green trousers. His morning breath is the mist in the valleys, and at evening there are stars in his eyes, a waxing moon over his shoulder, and the cool whisper of valley breeze in his voice. He comes this way to light the fires of autumn in the maple groves, to put a final polish on the late winesaps, to whistle a farewell to summer and set the foxes to barking and tell the owls that now they can ask their eternal questions.

October might be called a god of travel, if we were to fashion a new mythology; for now come the perfect days to get out and wander the hills and valleys of these latitudes. The scene changes from day to day, as though all the color in the spectrum were being spilled across the landscape—radiant blue of the sky and the lakes and ponds reflecting it, green of every tone in the conifers and in the reluctant oaks, yellows verging from sun simmer to moon orange in the elms, the beeches, the maples, and reds that range to purplish browns, sumac and dogwood and maple and oak and sour gum and sassafras and viburnum. There is the indigo of fox grapes, if you know where to find them.

October is colorful, it is exuberant, it is full of lively spirit. Spring fever can't hold a candle to October fever, when it comes to inner restlessness. The birds are on the wing, the leaves are footloose and eager for a breeze, the horizon is a challenge that amounts to an insidious summons. Listen closely and you can hear October, that fellow in the crimson shirt, whistling a soft melody that is as old as autumn upon this earth.

A TREE OF YOUR OWN

*E*verybody should own a tree at this time of year. Or a valley full of trees, or a whole hillside. Not legally, in the formal way of "Know all men . . ." and "heirs and assigns" written on a paper, but in the way that one comes to own a tree by seeing it at the turn of the road, or down the street, or in a park, and watching it day after day, and seeing color come to its leaves. That way it is your tree whenever you choose to pass that way, and neither fence nor title can take it from you. And it will be yours as long as you remember.

Red maples are beautiful trees to own that way. They color early and the color steadily deepens. Find one that turns mingled gold and crimson and you have a tree of wonders, for you never know whether another day will bring more gold or more rubies. It will be great treasure, in any case. And a sour gum is a thrilling tree to own, for its reds and oranges are like those of no other tree that grows. A dogwood, too, is one to consider, for it not only rouges itself with some of the warmest reds in the woodland; it decks itself with berry clusters that outstay the leaves, if the squirrels are not too industrious. Or you may choose the sassafras, and cherish the choice until all the leaves are fallen. For the sassafras is like a golden flame with all the warmth of orange and red and even purple mingled in. No fire that ever leaped on a hearth had the warmth of color that glows in a sassafras on an October hilltop.

Take your choice among them and many others. Make one your own, and know autumn in a tree that not even the birds can possess more fully. It's yours for the finding, and the keeping in your memory.

INDIAN SUMMER

If the Indians didn't call it Indian Summer—and the evidence indicates that they didn't—they certainly missed a good bet. If they had only named it they might have credit for one of the choicest seasons of the year, any year. But instead of naming it they seem to have enjoyed it as it came, getting in their harvest of corn and squash and putting by a haunch or two of venison. The name itself appears not to have been used until after the Revolution, in 1794, and then it was used by a Caucasian New Englander.

There isn't even any fixed date for Indian Summer. It comes in the fall, and that's about as close as anyone can come. Sometimes it comes in October, sometimes in November; sometimes it waits for the first hard frost—the black frost, as some call it—and sometimes it just appears over the hilltop and settles down while October is young and innocent. True, there are partisans who will insist that Indian Summer never can come this early; but even they can't set an arbitrary date. It isn't a calendar season. It makes its own rules.

The thing about Indian Summer, whenever it comes, is that it is so magnificently enjoyable. When it comes early it coincides with the best color of the year, the whole magnificence of maple and oak. Then it is doubly wonderful. When it comes late it relieves a dull and frosty November and makes us forget, for a little while, that winter is close at hand. Now and then—and this, too, can be argued—it comes twice in a year, both early and late. Such years are memorable. It could be that this will be one of those years. After summer drought and August and September hurricanes, maybe we deserve two spells of Indian Summer. We'll take the early one gladly, in any case, and hope for more.

THE FLOWERING WITCH

Witch hazel is in bloom now, the tufted yellow petals straggling like the unkempt hair of some blonde young witch. It is one of the few trees on which one can find leaves, flowers and ripening seed pods all together in the autumn. The leaves are now a rusty gold and ready to drift away, their year's work done. The seed pods are the result of last fall's flowers, and in the weeks to come they will pop open with uncanny force and fling their seeds twenty or thirty feet. And the flowers themselves are eccentric; not only are their petals like a tangle of little ribbons but staminate, pistillate and bisexual forms of the flower appear at the same time and even on the same twig.

Botanically, the witch hazel is *Hamamelis virginiana*, kin of the sweet gum tree. But the popular name goes far back and perpetuates the perfectly human tendency to revere the eccentric. For many generations a forked branch of the Hamamelis has been the favorite divining rod, or dowser, of those who claim and often seem to possess remarkable powers of locating underground water. Many a good back-country well still offers its sweet plenty as proof that a witch hazel branch, properly held in the right hands, could tell a man where to dig for water. This peculiar form of search for water was often called "witching" for water, and the bush from which the dowser was cut became a witch's hazel.

Where the "hazel" came from is anybody's guess. For witch hazel is no kin of the hazelnut or filbert, which belong to the birch family. But the witch hazel's bark and twigs yield an essence long used to ease sprains and bruises. According to some, witch hazel extract itself has elusive, witchlike qualities, somehow vaguely connected with the witch-hair blossoms that come in the autumn.

THE FESTIVE BERRIES

The winter berries light the woods and the roadside, unusually numerous and altogether festive. They garland the woods, and black alders make a gay display of vivid red along the roadside—holly red, for the black alder is *Ilex verticillata*, deciduous cousin of the familiar Christmas holly.

Flowering dogwoods bore many berries, most of which were stripped early, as always, by the eager squirrels. And the birds soon stripped the big crop of pokeberries and woodbine. Even the poison ivy had a fruitful season, which means only that the birds will plant more of the noxious vines along the old stone walls.

Deeper in the woods, the lesser berry plants had a good season too. The baneberries, both red and white, bore heavily and many of them still have their vivid berries. Checkerberry, the little plant with the big name, *Gaultheria procumbens*, and the tang of wintergreen and black birch, dangles its fat cherry-red fruits beneath its small canopy of evergreen leaves. And the trailing partridgeberry, *Mitchella repens*, seems to have been more fruitful than in years.

Some say the small berry plants, and the partridgeberry in particular, forecast the coming winter. Many berries, runs the belief, mean a cold, snowy season. The reasoning is backward, of course; many berries simply mean a favorable fruiting season just past. But there they stand—there they creep, rather, in the woodland beside the creeping pine and the Christmas fern, their berries like glossy little beads to decorate a tiny Christmas tree. Whatever the winter, partridges and their kind will have good eating when they most need it.

NOVEMBER WIND

*T*here is a gray wind to November, which whips the low scud across the sky and sends the last of the maples' color swirling through the woodland. Give it a bright day, and there is a silvery sheen to it; you can almost see it. Give it a dull day and it moans and whispers through the oaks, still brown with clinging leaves. Give it a chill day and it has a whetted edge.

It is a restless wind, almost as restless as the wind of March. But it roars and whistles over the hills from another direction. March wind sweeps up the valleys and over the hills, a rising wind almost as perverse as March weather. But November wind whirls down the valleys, with the weight of oncoming winter behind it.

Put rain in a November wind and it has the lash and bite of a sleet storm. Put a warm sun behind it and it is somewhat tempered, but you know it is only biding its time, waiting for reinforcements. At its best, you will never mistake it for the gusts of September or the breeze that comes with April.

The pines lean before it, and the dead branches of the oaks come crashing down. It strews the woodland with outworn litter, to be snow-buried and rotted into the soil whence it sprang. It piles icy waves on the headlands, to eat at rocky barriers and gnaw at the dunes. It flattens tall brown grass in marsh and meadow, and if the hills were less firmly anchored it would flatten them into the valleys. For it is a primeval force, the wind of November, one with the tides and the ice and the very spin of the earth itself.

THE HEARTH

There is this about a chill November: it makes one appreciate a fireside. And there is this about a hearth: it calls for small company, for companionship.

A hearth fire is a wasteful thing, in terms of economics. But so is much of the talk that generates beside an open fire, for it seldom settles big problems and it never pays the taxes. Much of it, like the heat from the logs on the andirons, goes up the chimney. But when you have said that, you have pretty well exhausted the case against the simmering log and the slow talk and the leisurely evening. And there still remains the reflected glow, which is its own excuse and needs no defense.

For there are times and occasions when quick heat and sharp words are among the world's largest inefficiencies. Some things, and friendships and understanding are high among them, mature best by ember-light and in a small company. It is doubtful that mob rule was ever inspired by the slow gleam of a fireplace. The tinder of violence and fanaticism requires a bigger fire and larger arena. Philosophy and faith are companions on the hearth, and ever have been.

There are better ways to heat a house, true, but neither love nor friendship is concerned too much with economics. Man built a home around his fire, and there the family grew. To his fireside he brought his friends, and friendship grew, and understanding. So hearth became home, and home became heart. And it has little changed over the centuries. What greater friendship than understanding? What deeper understanding is there than that which stands, back to hearth, and faces outer cold and darkness?

ICE GOSSAMER

Look to the little ponds if you would see the slow approach of winter now, the quicksilver waters between the brown hills that mirror ragged cattails and naked willows and the bright berries of black alder on their banks. At midday they mirror such late autumn silhouettes on their strangely calm surface, and under full moonlight in early evening they gleam with stars like an inverted sky. But come upon such a pond in early morning and the first touch of winter is upon it.

Frost lines the cattails and beads the floss straggling from their brown thumbs. The bright berries of the black alder are doubly red against the frosty branches of the bush, Christmasy in their brilliant contrast. Pines that stand at the water's edge are crisply green among the leafless maples. And on the water itself are the long, sharp ice needles which in the night's late hours have been knitting the intricate pattern of crystal that gleams in the morning sun. A few hours of sunlight, a few hours of wind ripples, and the fine tracery will be gone again. But in the dark of another night the cold needles will knit again; and each night they will knit more and stronger, until the whole pond is covered.

You see it now in its beginnings, a film so delicate it shatters in your hand as you try to lift a fragment from the water. It is the ice gossamer of November's end, fine as spider web, transient as a snowflake. It is the frost pattern of winter's breath on the crystal pools that lie cupped in the hollows of the long, starlit night.

FROST AND SNOW

The heavy frosts have come, and the first light snows have come and gone. The earth in these latitudes enters its season of cold dormancy. Down in the ground lie the corded roots and the fat corms and bulbs of green life, torpid and waiting for the summons of another spring. Over them is spread the blanket of leaves and stems and grasses, fall's natural cover of protection. But the real cover is yet to come, the snow that will temper the bitter depths of cold.

Snow may be a nuisance, but it is one of nature's best insulators. Those who live in the lands of long, cold winters welcome snow, knowing that when it banks their houses they are relatively safe from the coldest blasts that blow. The cold they fear is that which clamps down before the snows have come; for that is the cold that strikes through walls and drives its fangs deep in the earth.

It is the "open winter," as the farmers call it, the winter with little snow, that does the damage. When the ground lies bare, the frost drives deeper and deeper with each long night, heaving and scarring and killing. But give the earth even a few inches of snow at the turn of the year and the worst that January can offer will be shrugged off. Bury a bed of petunias under a snowdrift all winter, and they will hurry into bloom like hardy perennials, come spring. Give a field of winter wheat a blanket of snow and it will come to strong and early harvest.

In our order of living, snow has become a nuisance in city and town and on country roads. But the woods and the fields need snow, as always, if they are to weather our winters. Fortunately, the natural order of things brings frost, then snow, then the depth of cold. And nobody has yet repealed that order.

THE SILENT HINGE

The silence of December is upon us. There is no fly-buzz or bee-hum even on the midday air, no insect whir or rasp when evening comes. The wind may rattle the oak's dry leaves, but the sibilant whisper through full-foliaged trees is a midsummer memory. The dawn clamor of the crows no longer echoes, nor does the sweet matin song of the robin. Blue jays may jeer, but for the most part they go about their business in blue silence. The chickadee is the most vocal bird in the bushes, and his sweet notes have little strength or endurance—decibelly speaking, he can't begin to compete with a cicada or a katy-did. And they, too, at last are silenced.

The owl hoots among the hemlocks on a lonely hillside, and country dwellers may listen late to the finespun yapping of a fox. But their voices only punctuate the silence, which lies deep in the valleys where frogs, not so long ago, thumped the darkness. Even the streams are muted, their current slowed by frost in the ground at their beginnings and ice fringing their quiet pools.

The woodchuck sleeps. Chipmunks doze in their fluff-lined beds. Gray squirrels go chatterless about their treetop rounds. The silent rabbit even avoids the rustling leaf.

December's sounds are earth sounds and the sound of the chilling wind, the slow, cold pelt of winter rain and the swish of driven snow—and, where the cold strikes early and bites deep, the crack of expanding ice and the groan of rocks slowly riven by the silent frost. The waning year does not creak on its hinges.

WINTER SPECTRUM

From leaf-fall to first snow we think of the outdoor world, in these latitudes, as a drab and colorless scene, for our eyes are still remembering October and our hearts remember June. But late fall has its own spectrum, of browns and grays and conifer greens. We begin to recognize that narrower spectrum when the snow comes with its sharp accents. Then the browns stand out, separate from the grays, and the greens of pines and hemlocks and spruces come into their own. Even the bronzed grass and the weed stems of the fields reveal new color to the freshly perceptive eye.

Until snow comes, the elms at the roadside loom black against the sky. Against a white background their clean boles are all subtle browns and grays. The old apple tree is only a dark tangle of branches until a shimmering background reveals its winter motley, not one shade of brown but at least a dozen. On the hillside, doubly emphasized by snow and the bold white strokes of the birches, the pasture cedars are a brownish-green, a brown that verges on the ruddy shade of their own bark. And the heads of the leaning birches have a reddish cast, up where their twigs become a brush against the sky.

Look across a meadow, snow-dusted, and the range of tans and browns and bronzes is amazing. The bronze of the upland grass, the rusty stems of the ever-curving goldenrod, the oat-straw gold, the cornstalk tan, the clean ruddy red, all are there, and even tobacco brown and buckskin tan, in the frosted grass clumps and the bold seed heads. The colors are there; they have not gone. The spectrum may be narrow, but there is infinite variety, once leaf-fall is forgotten and the winter world has its own background.

FIRST SNOW

First snow should be a damp, clinging snow dropped from the skies with little wind; and it should come in the night. Then we waken to a world properly dressed for winter, with the white accents everywhere but without a muffling blanket of white. That should come later.

First snow should line the trees, so that when you look down from a hilltop you can see the intricate design of a venerable elm or an ancient oak, each limb and branch outlined in white. A stone wall should be a pattern in gray and white; and the stems of goldenrod should be graceful curves of white, half-scrolls quickly drawn as with a sketcher's crayon. Pines should bow formally, their green twice as green against the snow that clings for a brief time in their needle tufts. And blue jays should be brilliant in the little snowstorms they jolt loose when they come arrogantly to perch a moment in the apple tree.

There should be morning sunlight to gleam on the transformed world and give it a proper dazzle, for this is new, this is fragile loveliness. It cannot last. The wind will twist through the trees, even a gentle wind, and it will bend the goldenrod and sway the pine; and there will be little snowstorms from all the branches in the woodland. Then the snow will be underfoot, to melt and slush and crust among the fallen leaves, and seep away.

But for a little while there will be the tracery of this first snow on all uplifted things, and there will be a bright magic to the world. For this is first snow, full of wonder and beauty and softly frosted loveliness.

LOST FRAGRANCES

Go to the warm, dry attics of some country places and you will meet a fine old fragrance, the smell of drying herbs. Sage, and rosemary, and thyme; garden herbs, principally, perhaps with the tang of garlic, the pungence of dill, the sweetness of lavender. Thus we preserve, on a small scale, the old arts of the herbalists. But seldom will you find among those attic herbs the old stand-bys from the open field, for the old art and the old knowledge of useful wildlings fade away or vanish in the laboratory.

Who gathers yarrow today to dry and steep for a stimulating tonic? Who dries hoarhound to brew a tonic tea? Boneset once provided a hot infusion relied upon to break up a cold or ease malarial fever. Boneset still grows in every open field, but as a weed now, not a herb. The wild cherry can be found in most woodlands, but almost no one gathers its bark to dry and steep for a mild sedative. Pennyroyal once provided a remedy for colic. Who uses it now, fresh from the field? And dittany—once it was said to cure "anything in anyone." Dittany now is all but forgotten as a herbal remedy.

Unknowing, we get some of the more effective of the old herbs from the drugstore now, under new names and with new odors. Science catches up with the old arts, even though it may leave some of the trappings behind. And there is no doubt that science makes even the best of the old herbalists look like fakers. But what sweet-scented memories can be roused by a shot of penicillin? There was a time when even the smell of boneset tea could cure a mild cold. Can the smell of antihistamine do that? Never!

SAW LOGS

The upcountry farmer getting saw logs out of his wood lot this week is timing it just about right. It's mid-January and the moon is in the last quarter. Those logs will be seasoned to make good lumber, straight planks and flat boards.

In the old days, when most farmers cut their own saw logs, you didn't mean that lumber had been dried out when you said it was seasoned; you meant that it had been cut in the right season. And the season was governed by the moon as well as the month. Timbers cut during "the old moon of January"—sometimes they said February—would always stand straight and true. But if you cut your logs "when the moon is new to full, timber fibers warp and pull."

Such sayings were typical of a time when a countryman equipped with only an axe, an auger and a knife could build, furnish and equip a house from the trees in his own clearing. Wood was his most versatile material, and what he didn't know or learn about it wasn't worth knowing. When he began to build with sawed lumber, he carried this knowledge right into the sawmill and back, with the boards, to the building site.

The old houses and the old barns prove that the men who chose the lumber knew what they were doing. It's still good lumber, true and straight, after all these years. How much the moon's phases had to do with it can only be guessed, but there's no denying that the wood was seasoned to perfection in almost every case.

Farmers are essentially practical people and no more superstitious than city folk. But if a man wanted to get out a few saw logs for his own use he certainly couldn't be blamed for looking at the calendar first—a calendar with the moon's phases clearly marked.

WOLF MOON

Indians called it the Wolf Moon, knowing well the time when fangs were eager and hunger drove the pack. Most of the wolves are gone but the fangs remain, fangs of ice and cold, the great primal forces of winter's depth. The wind courses the valleys and harries the hills, and the long nights sharpen its fang. The ice lies deep.

In some lands there are mountain barriers to the winter wind; but our geography has no such design. Our mountain chains, for the most part, lie with the wind which moves down from the north. The great valleys merely funnel the gales so that they howl unfettered and roar across the flatlands until they have worn themselves out. Our winter winds have few barriers. Even the trees stand naked, to sigh and moan as the wind whips through them, freighted with snow or ice or merely freighted with cold. And the hills lie open to the elements.

Ice sheathes the ponds and clogs the streams. It thrusts at the banks with its own fangs. But more than that, ice gnaws at the hills. It thrusts a hidden fang into the granite of the hilltop and rips the rocks apart. Ledges that can defy all other elements crumble away beneath the ice, which can come from as impalpable a thing as a wisp of mist or as fragile a thing as a snowflake. Ice, the sharpest fang of all, and the most persistent.

The Wolf Moon, they called it, listening to the howl of the pack in the winter valleys. And the howl we hear tonight will be the wolf howl of the wind in those same valleys, the voice of primal forces at work in the winter world.

WINTER TREES

Winter strips the trees to their essentials. They stand now in bare bones, except the pines and spruces, and you can see what stands behind their graceful summer shapes.

That elm against the sky, which in midsummer is a great green feather duster—see how its sturdy trunk divides some distance from the ground, and divides again and yet again. It reaches upward, widening like an inverted cone, and all its branches point toward the sky.

Across the way is a scarlet oak. It has a trunk three feet through, and your eye can follow that trunk to the very top of the tree. But its branches start not ten feet from the ground, and they reach toward the horizon. Here's a tree broad as it is tall, and rounded, even in leafless winter, like a great dome.

The ash, whether white or black or red, is essentially a tapering trunk with whorls of lesser limbs—a pole with slender branches, now; a svelte and graceful tree in full leaf.

Maples tend to branch like the oaks, but with less spread and more lift. The sycamore, which shines as though perpetually frost-coated, divides like the elm and branches like the maple, and reaches out in all directions. The tupelo, or sour gum, is a central stem with a hopeless tangle of branches crisscrossed on each other, a veritable confusion of a tree without its leaves.

But of all, perhaps the most beautiful against the winter sky is the little flowering dogwood, with its horizontal limbs that reach skyward at the tips and form a fine lace pattern with their twigs. The dogwood is a picture tree, summer or winter.

PATIENCE

February rain isn't any wetter than that of March, and February snow isn't any colder or slushier than the snows of January. Nor is the sun actually summer-hot on an occasional mild and balmy February day. They just seem that way because, at this time of year, our weather nerves are right up on the surface. The bad seems worse and the good seems better than reality. We would give anything for a fine spring-fever week and a little sunburn. And down in our hearts we know we aren't going to get it—not yet.

It sometimes seems that our forefathers, who lived closer to the soil and the seasons, were a little more patient. In public print they wrote of February: "Now comes the deepest snow; now we receive the remainderment of winter." But look at their private letters and you see another picture of them: "February is a miserable time. I would gladly pass it by. . . . I long for March, inclement as it often is." And in their journals you will find laconic weather records that make chilly reading indeed, cold and wet and disappointing.

They, too, got winter-weary. They had their troubles, and they were impatient about them, down in their hearts. But, partly because they lived close to the land and understood the leisure of the changing seasons, they put up with them and saw them through. Spring was not only relief from winter; it was work, hard work and long hours, planting for the summer's growth. No year, no season, with without its pains and worries. But there was comfort in the knowledge of change, and even security. No troubles lasted forever, nor did any weather, good or bad. Winter ended, eventually, and spring came. And thus it is and always will be. And in that knowledge they lived out their winter-weariness, even as we shall live out ours.

GREEN FINGERS

There are robins in the lower part of the Shenandoah Valley, and once you cross narrow Tennessee and reach northern Mississippi you find daffodils beginning to bloom. Spring creeps north, already well established down along the Gulf. As you go on south, after seeing the first daffodils, the mockingbirds become more numerous and more sassy, and by the time you reach Mobile they are practically mad with song. By then you are in azalea country, with blossoms everywhere.

To the Northerner, it is enough to find blossoms and to smell the young, new season. But to those who have watched those blossoms open bud, the rains of this season have been an annoyance. Repeatedly one hears the wish, "Oh, if it would only fair up!" And one wonders how much "fairing" it takes to make a spring, once the flowers have come.

The streams are bank-full and red with mud. Country roads are quagmires. But oats and clover are green, and maples are turning crimson with their own buds opening. And on a few hilltops farmers are turning the soil. There's plowing to be done, between rains, if a crop is to be made next summer. A man can't sit all spring and wait.

It's an early spring to the outlander, a wet spring to the native. But it is spring, new and young and full of strengthening growth. You have to go south to find it, but it meets you halfway. Turn your back on it for a few days and it touches another hill to the north with its green fingers, warms up another valley, outdistances your eye. That's spring for you.

FLOWING WATER

The streams run faster now, and they leap and sing at midday. Water is still black, no matter how clear it may be, the black of contrast with icy banks where snow still lies. But it is live water, refusing now to be confined by ice. And it is carrying away, hour by hour, the deep frost of the cold night.

Walk beside a stream and you will feel the tang of sharp air morning and evening; but when the sun rides high you will know that there is warmth ahead. Here is movement, the surge of forces that will be livening all the earth in a few more weeks. Even the trickles that seep from beneath the drifts on a sheltered hillside are live waters, the sustenance for buds and shoots that await a warmer sun. The reluctant ice is eaten away. The earth itself gives up its frost to the waters that make their steady way down all the seams and crevices towards the valleys where brooks become rivers.

There is even the movement of waters across the marshland, a slow flow that creeps among the reeds and eases past the root-tangles of willow brush. It is there, in the sluggish waters, that spring will first come; for somehow the marshes generate their own vernal warmth. Frogs' eggs will lie milky in the pools, and skunk cabbage will spread its leaves, and dogtooth violets will put forth their mottled foliage.

But such matters are for later. Today the waters ooze and flow, and the ice recedes. Not until tomorrow will the leaf begin to reach and the root send up its shoot. Today the waters are alive and moving. That is enough for now.

SAP-RISE

The sap has begun to rise, and neither snow nor cold is going to stop it now. It has begun to work its way slowly up from the deep roots along the stems and trunks of bush and tree and out into the branchlets, where the tight-furled buds wait. You see it in the willows and the osiers, those red-stemmed cousins of the dogwood. The weeping willows show it best, among the willows; they glow with an amber gleam, as though some golden fluid had begun to course their inner bark. See a weeper against a dark hillside and it is a lively fountain, almost sunny, without a hint of leaf. Its twigs and withes have come to life again.

Along the river banks and in the lowlands there is the new ruddy glow, rich red, of the osier bushes. Two months ago they were a dead red-brown, waiting out the winter. Now they have the lively color of a deep ruby, a color that suffuses the whole stem. It is almost the color of the flowering dogwood leaf in October. In May these bushes will put forth bright green leaves, and in June they will have inconspicuous little yellowish-green flowers, and in September there will be lead-gray berries. But all this is yet to come, and the livening of the stems now is only a promise, a vivid promise there on the riverbank.

Sap rises in the other trees and bushes, but less spectacularly. The sassafras begins to turn green on the twigs, still a dusty, half-hearted green. Sugar maples are in full flow up in the snowy woods. Break a sumac stem and there is a faint ooze where a month ago there was no ooze at all. For the juices of spring have begun to quicken, to move, to make their way upward out of winter.

THE WINDS OF SPRING

February does not end; it frays away, or is blown away, into March. That is another way of saying that without a calendar we wouldn't know which was which, during this period of pause between seasons. What is another day, more or less, when March follows right on February's heels? One year that day belongs to February, and the next year it is a part of March; and the variation doesn't alter the arrival of the vernal equinox one whit.

Even the equinox, the one fixed point of the season, does not serve as anything but an index of daylight and darkness. It will come three weeks hence, and the roots and buds will know the change. But February a year ago went out on a wind with a ten-degree temperature, and the first week of March was full of snow and slush and shivers. This year February ends with daffodils up six inches, in these parts, and crocuses in bloom.

Travel west beyond the Mississippi, however, and winter still lies deep upon the land, such a winter as no man can remember. An end to February will be welcomed there with heartfelt thanks, if only because the March sun is a little warmer, the March wind not quite so sharply fanged. The snows should begin to melt, in March, and the blizzards to abate. And after March comes April, when winter is surely over—April, and green grass where the drifts lay deep, and new calves for the depleted pastures.

We have seen February, this year, from only one side. February has smiled upon us. Another week of it and we might have grown smug. So let it fray away and turn into March, and let spring come officially. The winds of spring are already blowing over the waiting hilltops.

SUGARIN' TIME

Maple sap was running ten days ago, and the syrup and sugar makers were exulting over an early run. The smell of wood smoke under the kettles and pans began to drift down from the Berkshires and beyond and, to the west, from the Catskills. With it, of course, was the tang of the syrup itself. Then came cold air out of the north, ushering in March, and the sap stopped flowing. The syrup makers had to wait. Wait for mild days, days at least when the temperature got above freezing. It takes chill nights and warm days to move the sap in a maple tree.

Maple sap comes from the tree clear as spring water. It has only the faintest taste of sweetness, and no visible color unless one could call its brightness a color; for it almost gleams, with a kind of crystalline clarity which must come from the trace of yellow or amber that lies somewhere in it. It takes from twenty to forty gallons of sap to make a gallon of syrup, depending on the season and the trees. And it takes a good deal of wood under the kettles, for all that excess water must be boiled away. So the woodland, at syrup time, is full of steam as well as smoke. And the syrup makers, after a day or so, have that fine, smoky smell of a ham just out of the smoke house.

There are easier ways to make syrup, of sorts, but there is no other way to make *maple* syrup. It is the essence of the maple tree, as full of color as the tree itself in October. It is sunlight and snow-melt and a spring day. And something more besides, for it is also maple woods and sap buckets and steamy kettles and smoky fires. It is up-country America in early spring, and you can taste it in every drop you put on a waffle or a pancake.

SUCCESSION

There is a succession in the days, now, that quickens the human heart. Whether they are gusty days or days of calm, chill days or days of deepening warmth, they have the air of change. No two days are alike. Sometimes it seems as though the season were trying a variety of moods, play-acting in a dozen different parts, eager to be spring and reluctant to be no longer winter. But the very indecision is itself the mark of change.

The hardy plants of spring reflect the trend. Daffodils are well up and hyacinths have broken ground. Crocuses have spread the color to the temperamental winds. Beneath their mulch, the peonies are showing pips of crimson. Flower buds are so fat on the forsythia that when a shoot is brought indoors its golden bells open almost overnight. Iris sends up its green bayonets. And mountain pink is full of fat buds awaiting only a few successive days of April sun. There is the amber glow, luminous and almost translucent, in the willow withes.

You walk through the garden, still largely bare and waiting, and you see these things. And you look down a long hillside and you feel them, feel the pressure of succession, the slow but certain urge of change. Growth is there in the earth, at the grass roots, at the twig ends. The green world is waiting, already in the making where the mysterious chemistry of sap and chlorophyll has its origins. And the heart responds, already sensing the seedling, the new shoot, the summer's dappled shade. April whispers from the hilltop, even as March goes whistling down the valley.